You *CAN* Be a WRITER!

24 OBSTACLES YOU CAN OVERCOME

Edward Gold

Printed in the United States of America
ISBN 978-0-9972437-6-5

Book design by CSinclaire Write-Design

Thank you to Juan Arango
for his in-depth editing of this book.

TABLE OF CONTENTS

Introduction

I believe that everyone has a story to tell, be it short or long. **The first step to getting your own story published is to write it.**

I know that sounds simple and for some people it is. I am not one of those people. I get distracted easily, my family and job consume my free time and I find it difficult to sit down and create after a long day when all I want to do is relax. I am also a perfectionist and a procrastinator, two things which can stop you from completing a book. And, on top of that, I have many ideas competing for my time. So many, in fact, that I start most of them and move on before finishing them. I have a lot of unfinished stories waiting to share with the world.

Does any of that sound like you? So, how did I beat all those obstacles and actually complete a book? Let me give you a little of my history.

I'm in my forties now. I've been writing for most of my life. I can't remember a time when I didn't dream of being a writer. I had good years where I wrote incessantly and bad years where I wrote next to nothing. Honestly, there were probably more bad years than good ones, but the dream was always there in the back of my mind.

Over the years, I've published a handful of poems and won several short story contests but I've never really felt like a published author because of them. I felt like they were just gimmes and not really deserving.

I've worked on literary magazines and newsletters, and I have been running a writers group for over eight years that now has over 1,500 members. And I have also been an assistant on another larger one for even longer.

I have had loads of opportunity and desire throughout my life. Then why now? Why have I finally completed and published a book? Why not twenty years ago? Why not ten? Why not even one?

I've held about twenty-two jobs in my non-writer career. Twenty-two. That's roughly one-and-a-half to two years per job. My shortest one was with Kirby Vacuum Cleaners selling door to door. That job lasted three days. I was jammed into a van with eight to ten chain smokers (I don't smoke!) for thirteen hours a day. I sold one vacuum, got my commission, and bolted. My longest job was around five years. I was a Presentation Specialist at a financial institution. I created presentations for bankers to help them close deals and secure money for the bank. I basically just made things pretty, but I loved it! It was creative, my co-workers were amazing and like family, and I could leave my work at the office with no stress of unfinished business—another shift would complete my unfinished jobs. Sadly, the bank downsized and laid off the entire department. I managed to obtain another position at the bank before my last day and have been in that position since. I don't love the job. It's okay but after coming from a position I loved and going back to another "eh" one didn't make me happy.

That has been my core driving factor to serious writing. I was tired of working at a job that doesn't make me happy and that benefits someone else instead of me.

Still, even with that core desire, I couldn't force myself to move forward. I was overwhelmed by the thought of self-publishing and marketing. Where do you start? Where do you sell your story? How do you format your story? How difficult is it?

Writing is hard. It takes work and patience. In this book, I will talk about obstacles I've faced, specifically as a writer, and how I've overcome them. A lot of the obstacles in this book overlap and are intertwined with each other as are some of the solutions. There are no blacks and whites, only shades of grey. I'll talk about some of my solutions but they are in no manner the only ones available to you.

They've helped me and they are still helping me. Overcoming an obstacle once does not remove or destroy the obstacle. **Obstacles**

are a constant war that you will be fighting forever. Like any war, some battles you will win and some you will lose. Maybe one day your favorite television show wins but on another you turn off the TV and knock out several hundred words. Just keep fighting. Don't give up.

Hopefully, this book will help alleviate your own fears, give you some ideas, clear up some of the mental clutter, and get you out there publishing your own stories.

Edward Gold

1
Self-Esteem

I have a low self-esteem with its roots extended far back into childhood. Just knowing about it isn't enough though. I fight this issue every day in nearly every aspect of my life. It is no surprise then that it has also affected my dreams of becoming a published author.

My low self-esteem probably leads directly to my perfectionism (which will be covered later in this book). When I produce something, I try to make it the best I can most of the time. I bring this up because even though I try to produce quality things, I still feel as if they aren't good enough. Even though I get lots of praise, I think to myself "Could I have tried harder and done better? Did I mess something up that someone will point out to me later? Do people like it or are they just placating me?"

That last question is an interesting one. Should I really care if someone doesn't like it? No, I shouldn't worry about it. But I still do, and that is directly related to my self-esteem.

If you haven't listened to Anthony Robbins' *Creating Lasting Change* audio course, I highly recommend it. I've listened to the program several times now and each time I pick up something new and get totally psyched up about changing myself into what I want to be. One of the things Mr. Robbins talks about is the six basic needs that every person has: 1) Certainty/Comfort, 2) Uncertainty/Variety, 3) Significance, 4) Connection/Love, 5) Growth, and 6) Contribution.

A low self-esteem affects most of these needs. I'm not comfortable with or certain of my abilities even though history has proved otherwise. I don't feel significant most of the time. I don't always feel a true connection with other people, especially if they appear confident. I haven't grown or contributed enough because my subconscious tells me that it isn't worth it, that no one cares anyway. My intellect knows otherwise but my subconscious often rules the roost.

If low self-esteem is ingrained so deeply into your core being, how do you beat it? The only thing I know to do is to persevere; to trudge forward and hope for the best. **Push your fears back and ignore these feelings as much as you can. Trust that you have value to add for at least one other person.** Maybe your story could change one person's life. Look at Daniel Radcliffe, the boy who played Harry Potter in all eight movies. If J.K. Rowling had not written the *Harry Potter* books his life would be completely different. Your story could do the same for someone else.

2
Distractions

Life is a long series of distractions. It is rare to get away from them.

Marketeers know this. They go out of their way to distract you, to get you to notice and buy their products. That's how end-caps in department and grocery stores came about. As part of their revenue plan, marketeers purposefully put items to tweak your interest on those end-caps. They want to distract you from you shopping trip and subtly urge you to buy those products, as well as to lead you down those aisles. That's also why they place candy bars and small odds and ends in the checkout lanes. They want to distract you into an impulse purchase.

Distractions attack you from all sides, all the time. They come in many forms: advertising, television, family, friends, Internet, email, and music to name only a few. Even a gorgeous day can be a distraction. I find it more difficult to be inside typing when it is nice outside rather than when it's raining.

So how do you beat distractions especially when you are being specifically targeted on a regular basis?

You have to work around them.

A lot of people **write in the mornings** before the rest of their family is awake and when they have fewer things competing for their time. Others write after their families have gone to bed. My best writing time is after 8:30pm at night. This is tough because I am also tired most of the time after long days of work and from having two kids under three years old at home.

Some people have a **separate computer dedicated to writing**. Often, these computers aren't connected to the Internet. They put it in a quiet room so they can concentrate and not be overwhelmed by external stimuli.

Others they take their laptops to a library or a coffee shop, **away from their regular haunts**. It is often easier to get distracted in a familiar environment.

My biggest distractions are movies and television. My day job and my writing time are mostly solitary so I like to hear the voices talking, plus I like the stories and action. If I put a show on first sometimes I am able to tear away from it later and write, but normally I lose that time to the distraction. I literally have to force myself to **put on other sounds first**, like ocean waves. I have to do this in the first few one or two minutes in order to stave off putting on a show. The longer I wait, the harder it is to choose a non-distracting sound over a show.

When is your best time to write? What is you ideal place to write? How can you limit things that might distract you?

3

Family

I love my family but they do consume a sizable chunk of my time. This isn't a bad thing. Family is important. I enjoy spending time with them and want to instill family values and help educate my daughters as well as have lots of fun. Still, playing chase or picnic and having "family adventures" (which is what we call family trips and outings) means that I can't write during those times.

The best way to write around your family is either in the morning before everyone wakes up or at night after everyone goes to bed. This way you can still spend distraction minimized, quality time with your writing. I am not a morning person. I am a night person. I've been up late every night for most of my life and I am just used to it and it allows me time to write late into the night.

I **use a voice recorder or jot down notes to remember things** that I think of during the day so that I can revisit them later. That helps a lot because sometimes I will get a eureka-flash during the day and if I forget to take note of it, the idea is lost. I have too many other things competing for my attention.

Sometimes you may get frustrated when you lack time to write. Depending on how important your family is to you, when you do get frustrated, try to **remember that your writing could help your family in the long run**. If you start getting residual income then you might be able to leave your job and find more time to spend with your family.

One of the best things you can do to **work with your family** instead of against them is to discuss your writing and dreams with them, that way they can help you if possible. Maybe they can help edit your story, come up with ideas or suggestions, or draw illustrations. At the minimum they can offer support and understanding.

4
Job

Probably everyone reading this book has a job - a place where you spend a good portion of your life trying to make money so that you can eat and have a place to live and own some creature comforts. You may be fortunate to like your job, you may not. Either way, it still eats into the time you can devote to your dreams.

There isn't a lot you can do about your job getting in the way. You could leave your job and commit to writing full time but that isn't truly feasible for most people.

One thing you can do is to **get away from your desk or station at lunch time and write**. I find that if I stay at my desk I still want to work for my job rather than for myself. One thing to think about is that, although necessary for most of us, a job is still furthering some-one else's dreams and not our own.

I also started a lunchtime writing group at work. We meet twice a week for half an hour. Our focus is on the writing not hanging out and talking, most of the time. Sometimes we end up chatting more than writing but it is still the commitment and opportunity that we need.

The other way to write around your job is to do it before or after you go to work.

5

Perfectionism

I am a perfectionist. Ouch! Bite my tongue. I'm not sure when it happened, but perfectionism is no longer a desirable trait in a lot of situations. It went the same way as "multi-tasking" did in the corporate world. Somehow they both picked up negative connotations, however I do concede the point. If you keep trying to make it perfect, it will never get done. You'll keep tweaking bits here and parts there and words over there. Some edits are good yet over editing can take all the life and excitement out of your story for both yourself and your readers. It also just postpones your future as a published author.

"Done is better than perfect." I heard this saying for the first time in the last few months during an event hosted by Chandler Bolt of *Self Publishing School* - I don't recall who said it originally. It's brilliant. I have it taped to my monitor at work and use it like a mantra when I find myself over-editing and over-tweaking to try to make it perfect.

I have news for you. **It will *never* be perfect.** And, if by some miracle you do manage to achieve perfection, some people won't like it anyway. That's just a fact of life. There are over 7 billion people on Earth. Billion. There is no possible way that you will be able to please them all.

On a bright note, you're just as likely to have as many fans as you do haters. If you've only got 3.5 billion fans instead of the full seven-count, I believe that you'd still be happy about that, and be making tons of money to boot.

I recently read an ebook that I thought was awful. When I went to post my review on-line, it already had about thirty reviews and they were all four and five stars. I actually re-read the book to see if I was wrong about it. No, I still didn't like it. My first thought was that the reviews were all by friends of the author but then I remembered that not everyone in the world sees things through the same filters as I do.

The point is that some people will like it, some won't, regardless of its perfection. I'm not saying "don't edit", I'm saying make it great, or even just good enough, and move on to your next story. **Done is better than perfect.**

6

Over-Preparation

I am one of the most over-prepared people I know. I've carried an umbrella to work every day for almost seven years and only used it a handful of times. Admittedly, it is a portable model that tucks into my lunch bag but I still have it with me. I over-prepare because I like having the answers and appearing knowledgeable and ready for anything. I feel like it allows me to make quicker decisions and adjustments when I need them later. As mentioned in Chapter 1, one of the Driving Needs that Anthony Robbins talks about is "significance". Being prepared is one of the ways I feel significant.

The problem comes in when you spend too much time preparing and not enough time doing. Several years ago, I noticed that this is exactly what I was doing. I'd even started getting ready to get ready to do something. My work would be amazing but it'd be late. Or I'd spend hours writing a MS Excel VBA macro that only saved me a few minutes of time every now and then.

I had started losing my now so that I would be ready later if something occurred. Not when, but if. I was preparing for possibilities instead of focusing on what was happening right now, which leads to missing a lot of opportunities. In essence, my over-preparing caused me more losses than gains, even though I was ready for some eventualities.

Like perfection, you'll never be able to be ready for everything. In preparation, watch some training videos, take some courses, expand your knowledge, learn a new word every day, but don't forget to stop and move yourself forward. You can watch all the training videos you want (I know, I've seen a lot of them and they are endless and relentless) but learning how to do something doesn't make it happen - you make it happen. **Stop preparing to be a writer and be a writer.** Just being aware of when you are over-preparing will help.

7
The "Right" Word

Has this ever happened to you? You are blithely typing along in your story and you get stuck on one word in a sentence. Your brain can't move past it until you've found the best word for that one spot. You know there is a perfect word but you just can't quite remember it.

You decide to do a quick Internet thesaurus search to find similar words. You look through the choices. Maybe you find the one you were looking for or even a better one, maybe not. Then you decide that as long as you are on the Internet anyway, you might as well do a quick email or Facebook check, you know, just in case something important has come up. Then you see an email that wasn't truly important but looked interesting so you opened it and followed the link inside.

The next thing you know, it is an hour later, you haven't accomplished any more writing, and you can't even truly recall your train of thought from when you were last writing. Now, starting to write again means refocusing your mind and creativity which can be hard work. Subconsciously you think, Work? No thank you. I've just been relaxing and enjoying myself for an hour. It's too much effort to start up again. I'll just start again tomorrow, when I have more time. Of course, the loss of time is your fault and you know it, but you tell yourself that you will be stronger tomorrow and that it won't happen again. But it does. Over and over again.

While trying to find that one perfect word you managed to waste lots of valuable writing time and also likely have set up a pattern to do it again. After all, browsing the Internet feels good and is easy; writing is hard work with less short term enjoyment.

I've worked in the financial industry for years and one thing that I learned was how to get past that one word or that one error and move forward. When a banker doesn't know exactly what word they want to use in a presentation they put it in brackets, which tells them that it isn't final and that they need to revisit it later when they have had time to think about it.

This is easily applicable to writing a book. **Instead of trying to find the perfect word every time, just put the word in brackets and move on.** I even use this for names that I am not sure I like. An example is: "When [Sue] approached Mark, she waved him away [uselessly]." I'm not sure that I like the name "Sue" for that character and "uselessly" may not be the best word to use either. Remember, done is better than perfect.

Yes, you still have to go back and revisit the bracketed words later but that uses less time than stopping your train of thought, figuring out that perfect word, and possibly losing hours of time due to distractions.

To sweeten this idea even more for you, I've found that I don't use brackets on a normal basis in any writing that I do, which means that **using a simple "Find" feature in any conventional software will quickly locate the words that I've bracketed**. Just search for "[" or "]". Bam! You're right at the spot that you wanted to revisit. Now you have given your brain time to work on the word and kept your train of thought moving in the interim. It doesn't get much sweeter than that.

8

Procrastination

This was a difficult chapter to start. I kept putting it off and putting it off because I imagined it would be difficult to write. When I actually verbalized that thought to myself, I realized that I was procrastinating writing the chapter on procrastination. That's pretty funny. Realizing what I was doing made me start writing this chapter, just so I could beat it and stop putting it off.

Procrastination means putting something off until later when you could, or should, be doing it now. It is one of the most difficult obstacles for me to overcome. Even as I write this, I have taken a break for several minutes to throw a ball for my dog, Loki. Does Loki need love and attention? Certainly. But so does my writing. Starting and then stopping again to throw a ball is an example of procrastination.

Procrastination can be difficult to manage because **you may not even realize that you are doing it**. For example, I host an Accountability Group as part of the writers' group that I run. Anyone who signs up has a certain word count that they need to hit each week. In order to make it more exciting for them I send a weekly report with statistics and running totals. One member suggested that my making the reports so complicated was me procrastinating from writing. That made sense to me so, in the next Group session, I minimalized the reports and tracked less information, giving me more time to write.

So, how do you beat procrastination? Like a lot of the obstacles in this book, the first step is recognizing when you are procrastinating. Then **start with small, attainable goals**. Small steps will still move you towards the finish line. If you don't take any action at all you will never finish. Maybe set a small daily word count goal, like 200 words. 200 words is only about three paragraphs. Easy. Or maybe your goal is to write for five minutes every day. Anyone can write for five minutes. The most difficult part is getting started.

There is a method that I have started using to help overcome procrastination that has netted me over 20,000 words in about two months. That is more than I have written in at least ten years combined. I talk about this in other chapters too. I've heard that this method started with Jerry Seinfeld. It is often called the "Don't Break the Chain" method.

The basis of his method is to use simple goals and simple, immediate visual feedback to move you forward towards your goals. For **every day that you meet your goal, put a big red "X" on that day on a wall calendar**. Hang your calendar somewhere prominent and highly visible. After a few days you will get a visual chain of red X's. You won't want to break the chain of red X's. It's visually motivating and a simple goal: get an X every day. Since the end goal is so simple it makes the more difficult goal of writing easier by extension.

I use a dynamic calendar that I have included for free on my website (see Appendix 2 for link). It is a one page printout and I left extra space on each day so you can record your word count if you want to track it.

My small goal is to write something towards actual content every day. I do not have a specific word count or time frame associated with the goal. My worst day was only 29 words, but it is still 29 more than I had the day before and I still got my red X. My best day was 2,165 words, which I never would've gotten if I hadn't written because I really wanted that day's X. As of writing this, I have 133 consecutive X's. 133 days of writing something every day. That alone is enough to motivate me to write something, just so I don't break my chain.

While I still procrastinate starting sometimes, this method inspires me to not postpone writing for more than a few hours or a day at most. You may have a few false starts where you break the chain. I had one myself. Just try again.

Another option to try is to **set a schedule and then keep it**. Keep it simple and uncomplicated. Maybe every day you can block off fifteen minutes at 6:00pm or 7:30am to write.

Anthony Robbins sums it up well when he states that procrastination "is the opposite of using your personal power. Procrastination is being immobilized. It is needing to do something and not following through. It is the silent killer because it grows on you. It just creeps along until pretty soon it has taken control of your life. Why do we procrastinate? We think that taking action will be more painful than not taking action."

Procrastinators tend to put off fixing their procrastination. Take a small action. Take it again. And again. And keep on taking it until it grows into a big action. And then keep on taking it until it transforms into a way of life.

9

Habits

I'm forty-five years old. I've had forty-five years to build habits. Some are good and some are bad.

Here are some examples of good habits:

I've been playing doubles sand volleyball on a regular basis for over twenty five years. It gets me outside, provides me exercise, and and I can share it with friends. I can physically and mentally tell when I haven't played in a week or two. I start to crave it and my body starts feeling yucky. My entire physiology changes.

I almost exclusively drink water and iced tea, and drink lots of it. I'm sure that I get more than the daily recommended amount by quite a bit. This is good because it fills my stomach so I am not as hungry and it also keeps me hydrated.

I read books to my daughters before every nap, before bed, and some-times randomly during the day. This practice is great because it not only gives me quality time with my children but it gives me insight into how to write children's books. It is also great for them because it builds their vocabulary and develops their own reading habits and listening skills.

Here are some examples of bad habits:

I eat when I watch a movie or television. This actually makes me hungry when I watch a movie with no intention of eating. My body has associated the two events so they trigger each other. I then eat a lot when I am not actually hungry, thus adding extra calories to my diet without always thinking about or experiencing what I am eating.

I don't count my drinks when I start drinking alcohol. I normally have a general idea but I don't really pay too much attention to it. This, coupled with the fact that I can drink very quickly (I can polish off 20 ounces in around ten seconds or less) can sometimes lead to the foot-in-my-mouth syndrome or other bad situations.

I am late to places by ten to fifteen minutes on a regular basis. It reflects poorly on myself and can show disrespect to others. I underestimate the time it takes me to get places. My wife once said that I think every place is "only fifteen minutes away" even though it could be twenty or twenty-five minutes.

Habits can be tricky. You might think you have a good habit but it may be a bad habit in disguise. For example, using my drinking lots of water habit. I had to actually cut back my consumption a little because I was drinking too much. I never realized my habit could be bad until I went to Africa for two weeks. I was told to avoid drinking the local water because it would cause diarrhea and other unpleasantness. However, after about two days of very limited water I started feeling sick from its absence. My body had gotten so used to loads of water that it didn't know how to handle such a drastic decline. I finally broke down and drank the local water for the rest of the trip. Fortunately, I didn't have issues but ultimately I had to change my habit somewhat to avoid a similar situation in the future.

Habits are ingrained into us by past events and emotions. What we experience shapes us. If something hurts us we find methods to avoid it. If something pleases us we find ways to recreate the good feeling. **The first step in changing your habits is to recognize them and decide if they are good or bad for you and your dream.** Why are you eating food at that particular time? Are you stressed? Is it linked to something else?

What habits can get in the way of writing? Watching television or movies is a big one. It is easy to fall into the habit of sitting down to relax after dinner and watching something rather than writing. Other bad habits may include browsing the Internet, constantly checking email, playing Candy Crush Saga or Minecraft. This is obviously not an exhaustive list.

In order to get rid of a habit you don't want you need to replace it with a new habit. Set small goals that will help you meet your larger goal. Instead of watching television directly after dinner, you could write for fifteen minutes and then watch your show if you are still interested. Fifteen minutes is not overwhelming. It is a small goal and easily obtainable. Once you start hitting that small goal every day it will become a new habit and then you can ramp it up a little more, maybe 30 minutes a day, and so on.

Take a look at what you are doing instead of writing. Are you doing it out of habit? They say it only takes thirty days to create a new habit. Let's get going!

10
Critique

Critiques are a good thing when approached the right way but sometimes they can also hold you back. Maybe someone read one of your stories and told you that they hated it. Ouch! That's painful.

People's natural inclination is to avoid pain. If their words hurt you then you may put you work aside to avoid the same pain in the future. Also, if this person disliked your work so much, it must be a piece of garbage, right? No! That is not right! It's possible but highly unlikely.

I'm going to share with you the worst critique I have received to date. I was writing a sci-fi story for a short story contest. I will defend my story a little by saying that there was a 1,000 word limit and I created an entire intricate world based on people made of glass and an assassins guild within that word limit. In order to cram an entire new world into 1,000 words I had to be brief and concise. It didn't leave a lot of room for development.

Here is the critique:

> *"There is a MASSIVE problem with this story, which renders it in my opinion almost a total failure (sorry for being so blunt, but I don't do you any favors by pulling my punches).*
>
> *Almost the entire story is narrated, described, summarized – the great lesson of writing is, of course, SHOW DON'T TELL. Well, you tell almost everything and show almost nothing. It's*

incredibly frustrating. I understand not wanting to lard your story with backstory and infodump, but what you end up with is almost an outline of a story instead of a completed, really satisfying read.

Starting with the second paragraph.

"He was never the child they wanted him to be" etc etc. "Normal glassies shied away from him" etc. Well, SHOW US ALL THIS HAPPENING! Show his parents rejecting him! Show the "glassies" shying away from him! Let us see this happen and figure it out for ourselves!

"if it weren't for the Night Society. They found him passed out" – SHOW THEM FINDING HIM! SHOW them inducting him! Show them training him in stealth! SHOW THEM GIFTING HIM WITH THE DAGGER!

"S'Dian cut back on his work" – SHOW ALL THIS HAPPENING! SHOW him and Flickering go out on their dates and fall for each other! Don't narrate it in the past tense – show it happening as it's happening!

"Their differences attracted them" - SHOW THIS! Let us figure it out instead of you telling us!

"S'Dian was called in for a high-priority assassination" – SHOW HIM BEING CALLED IN!

This really burns me, how much you narrate and summarize rather than show. Are you trying to keep your story from feeling padded? In fact, you're achieving the opposite effect – it seems artificial, it seems like fiction rather than real. Underwriting is almost as fatal an error as overwriting, and it's maybe harder to correct. As an editor, I can cut stuff out that doesn't belong, but only the writer can figure out how to put in stuff that should be there but isn't.

And you really need to. You've got half a story here – bad enough that you cut out the backstory, but you also cut out the entire heart and guts of the real story – the romance between S'Dian and Flickering. This is the heart of your story – the only reason we give a damn about S'Dian in the first place (why should we give a shit about a cold-hearted assassin?) and also the McGuffin of the plot – his falling for a woman dooms her, sort of a perverse version of Little Joe Disease. But we NEVER SEE HIM FALLING FOR HER – we find out about it after the fact because you tell us it happened, but you deny us the pleasure of SEEING it happen. That pisses me off.

All that said – the story itself is okay. Interesting setting, and I like that you never explain how the "glassies" come into being.

But you have to go back and fill in all the blanks. Otherwise, we're not really going to care half as much as we should about S'Dian and his chosen fate."

Wow! Talk about brutal. My first reaction was anger - how dare he? I had poured my heart into this story. I was hurt. Was it really that bad? Even now, I get agitated when I read this review although for different reasons. I get upset now because of his tone and presentation and how it makes me feel unworthy (even now) and nearly stopped me from submitting it to the contest back then.

After my hurt and anger phase of many weeks and re-readings, I finally got past the emotions and was able to understand what he was saying through his contempt.

I learned a lot from this one incident. I learned that there will always be someone, somewhere, who doesn't like your story and that some people will be nasty about it.

I also learned that there are always circumstances in any situation that not everyone understands as well as you, like my word count restriction. We all do the best we can when limited by circumstance.

Now I understand the difference between "show" and "tell" which, if you are involved with a writers' group, you have probably heard the phrase "show, don't tell" before. I had always found the concept difficult to grasp.

Knowing that I will likely never receive a review as harsh as this ever again is a great burden to have lifted since the worst feedback is probably behind me.

The critique of my story helped me tame my ego a bit as well. No matter how good I think it is, there will also be some room for improvement.

It showed me to always watch for the good feedback even if it isn't apparent right away.

It taught me the value of setting things aside for a while and then coming back to them when your mind is in a better place.

And, this also taught me how <u>not</u> to word my critiques to other people when they ask me to read their stories.

You are certain to get both positive and negative reviews and critiques, especially since everyone reviews everything now. While some of them may sting, **try to see the good in them and don't let them dictate your future.** Find the good in them, or the lesson, and use that to make yourself stronger.

So what happened to my story? Did it win the contest? No, but the contest judges wrote back to me personally. They indicated that it had been short-listed, even though it didn't win first place. Then they went even further and discussed why it didn't win, as well as pointed out what they liked best.

Here is an excerpt from that letter:

> *"Your story was well-written, and your use of the theme was strikingly unusual. You dressed a familiar plot in shining new form; the description of the glassies at the carnival was particularly striking and attractive... I'm sure I'll see your name again, in professional magazines, other genre venues and maybe next year's contest!"*

It is rare to get any feedback from contests and submissions - they are just too busy to respond to every submission. So, I felt like a winner, even though I didn't win the contest.

If I had let that first, negative, critique be the final word I might have never submitted it to the contest. That negative feeling would have effectively killed the story for me.

11

Motivation

We all have really long and difficult days in our lives - stress at work, screaming or crying kids, migraines, deaths, arguments, car accidents, and injuries. These events, and more, all contribute to wearing you down each day. I find it difficult to sit down and create stories after a long day when all I want to do is relax and have a beer.

I've heard that **you only have a certain amount of energy every day**, kind of like an energy bank. You make withdrawals all day long and when your funds are depleted you have nothing left. Once that supply is gone you have no energy left to spend on your writing. You can't even muster the energy to be motivated about writing.

This is why **a lot of writers find that first thing in the morning is their most productive time to write**. They still have energy and focus, plus morning writers have the added benefit of fewer distractions since everyone else is still asleep.

I'm not a morning writer. I'm not a morning person. I never have been. I'm normally go to bed around 12:30 or 1:00am every night and then get up again at 6:45am with my kids. Then I head off to work around 8:45am and get home again around 5:30pm. After dinner and putting the kids to bed, it is then 8:00 or 8:30pm before I can get to my computer to write. Some days it is an hour or two later because I spend extra time with my wife. Most days, by that time, my reserves are gone and I am wiped out. If I try to watch any kind of show right away, I completely lose motivation to write. I am officially overloaded for the day. I persevere, sometimes nearly asleep in my chair, because

I know it is the only time I have where I am not bombarded by life. Some days it is sheer willpower that keeps me going. The motivation I have to write under those conditions comes from several places.

First, I can be obstinate. I don't like to give up on a problem. Second, after I've written just a little bit I feel better and more motivated to write even more. I know this from past experience and that makes starting easier.

I heard somewhere that being motivated at the beginning of a task is more difficult than staying motivated to finish something.

Take jogging for example. The actual physical act of starting your legs moving to jog three miles is a lot more difficult than finishing the three miles. Once you have started you are less likely to give up, and more likely to finish. So, instead of focusing on the three mile goal, focus on standing up. Then focus on putting on your shoes. Then focus on going out the door. All of those are small, easily attainable goals, and they advance you towards the larger goal without overwhelming you by focusing on the larger, more formidable goal. And you are taking an action rather than putting it off.

The same is true for writing. Let's say that you want to write a novel. If the average novel is 70,000 words and you are at word zero... holy moly! That feels enormous! So, instead of focusing on how far you have to go, focus on sitting down. Then focus on writing a few words, maybe only a few sentences. **Small steps still move you towards the finish line; if you don't take action you will not move forward.**

Third, I want to get my red X so I don't break my chain. I talk about **Don't Break the Chain** in the chapter on procrastination. I've found that a lot of the obstacles we have as writers overlap, as do the solutions. Don't Break the Chain works because it is simple and visual. There is a link to the calendar I use at the end of the book.

I've also found that **watching writer-interviews or help videos and tutorials helps to motivate** me. There are a lot of good videos on the Internet that you can use to pump yourself up for writing and publishing. Some of the writer's videos and content I follow are by

Joanna Penn, Joseph Michael, James Clear, Tara Lynne Groth, Jeff Goins, Chandler Bolt, Jon Bard, and Bryan Harris, yet there are many others with quality content. While they don't talk about motivation specifically, what they talk about motivates by example. Yes, they may try to sell you something, they are trying to make a living too. I am not pushing you to buy anything, just suggesting that you watch, learn, and get motivated by people that inspire you. If you purchase anything that is entirely up to you.

Another good way to get motivated and to stay motivated is to join a critique group. Critique groups are good sounding boards for your work and often offer supportive and constructive feedback or praise. Once you can see that other people appreciate your work, you'll be more excited to keep working on it.

There are many other ways to get motivated, like treating yourself to something once you hit a goal, or exercising which gives you energy and pumps blood into your brain for more creativity. Try several things until you find a method that works for you.

12

Emergencies

Everyone will always be affected by an emergency at some point during their life. Maybe a family member dies, or a child gets sick, or you get in an accident, or have a flat tire. All of these events will take away from your writing.

However, there isn't much you can do about them except cope and continue. I don't expect anyone would ignore their emergencies in order to write, especially if it is an emotional emergency like a death. Not only will you be drained emotionally but writing will likely be the furthest thing from your mind.

Still, **writing could actually help in the healing process for you**. You could write a letter or a journal entry about your emergency and feelings. That might help you cope, as well as keep you writing in some fashion.

If that doesn't work for you, handle your emergency as best as possible and just remember your long term goal of being a writer. **If you keep your goal in mind, when you are ready to write again it will be a lot easier** to write those first words and all the words that follow them. The Don't Break the Chain system could help you get started again or even keep you writing at a minimal level while your life gets back to normal.

13

Boredom

This chapter is about boredom with your story, not boredom in general though the same principles apply. Boredom occurs because you aren't doing something that excites you.

Let's say that you are watching a television show or a YouTube video and you start to get bored with it. What do you do?

Option one is to soldier on and continue watching in hopes that it gets better in an attempt to justify the time you've already spent on it. The chances are good that you will remain bored and your mind sluggish.

Option two is to change the channel or video to something else. Have you ever watched television with a channel surfer? Flip. Flip. Flip. Pause. Flip. It takes them time to find something that interests them and doesn't bore them.

A third option would be to get up and do something else entirely which, honestly, is probably the best option but I think there are only some of us that do that on a regular basis. I'm not normally a third option person. I'm more of an option two person.

Now, let's see how applying that same situation to writing a novel produces the same three options. There you are, writing your master-piece at 500 words an hour and suddenly your speed slows to a crawl and you can't seem to think of what to write next. I propose that this is because you are bored with what you are writing.

I've found that sometimes I can write 2000 words in only a few hours and other times I only get 500 words in that same time frame. I started paying attention to why this was happening. Invariably, the piece I was working on was boring. There wasn't much action, or it didn't excite me or it was a transition from one action sequence to another, more filler than plot.

Once I realized why I was having this problem I solved it by simply moving on to **write a different scene** instead (option two), rather than forcing myself to complete the scene (option one). Rather than plugging along slowly on something unproductively, I would still make progress on my book but just not linearly. It does, however, take a little getting used to writing a story out of sequence.

One writing tool that I found that helps to write this way is *Scrivener* by Literature and Latte. *Scrivener* is a software program developed specifically for writers and makes non-linear writing a breeze. If you have never heard of Scrivener before, I suggest you check it out (see Appendix 2 for link). You can download and use the full, unlimited software free for 30 days, and the 30 days is not linear/consecutive. It is 30 actual/non-consecutive days (Ha! I never realized until right this moment that Scrivener's free trial program is probably a foreshadowing of the product itself. I love it!).

Scrivener does not come without its drawbacks, however. The largest is that it is complicated to learn since there are lots of options and features. You can search the Internet for help but the best place I have found for help with Scrivener is Joseph Michael's *Learn Scrivener Fast* program (see Appendix 2 for link). I don't normally purchase on-line training programs because I can normally figure it out for myself, but I purchased his Ninja Program and have already learned so much. I believe it is totally worthwhile if you want to learn *Scrivener*.

When I do leave a boring section for a more exciting one, I **try to stay in the same story most of the time since switching between stories can sometimes inhibit your thinking process**. A story about a serial murderer causes you to think along completely different lines than, say, a story about a bunny rabbit.

You'll eventually have to write those skipped pieces but maybe you'll be in a better mental state when you get back to them. It's also possible that you'll discover that you don't need some of those passages in the story anymore. You may realize that they don't benefit the story, so you may decide to skip them altogether.

I've spent some time thinking about boredom with my own stories and what it could mean. If I am bored writing something, won't my readers be just as bored reading it? And, maybe, by extension, the entire book may be boring. Is it? Would I be better served by moving on to another book entirely? Only you can decide that for your own stories.

14

Sensory Deprivation

Wat I mean by sensory deprivation is lack of stimulus while you are writing. I find is much more difficult to write in a completely silent setting than in one with some background noise.

I expect this is because our culture has evolved to a constant-stimulation state. We are connected to background stimulation almost twenty-four hours a day, seven days a week. I even find it difficult to sleep if I don't have the hum of the ceiling fan.

Perhaps you are one of those people who can write better in complete silence. That's great! If you are like me though, you're more productive with some kind of background noise.

I solved this issue by **finding some background videos, music, or sounds that help me concentrate which don't distract me too much**. I use recordings of people talking in bars, ocean waves, forest sounds, familiar music from my computer, and often videos of nature settings.

I use familiar music because my mind already knows the songs and I can actually sing along without interrupting my train of thought. I use my own files and CDs so that I don't get distracted by commercials.

I like using nature videos too because not only do they offer auditory stimulation but I can glance over and see relaxing nature when I need a slight break. There is a series that aired on TV some time ago called *Sunrise Earth*. If you can get hold of that series, it is perfect background noise for writing. There are no commentators. It is fifty-plus hours of relaxing sounds, beautiful nature-scapes, and worldwide sunrises broken down into hour-long chucks. This is a series that I use regularly and highly recommend.

You can also search YouTube for "relaxing nature sounds" and get hours of mostly commercial-free streaming video. You can even find a few of the Sunrise Earth episodes there.

You'll need to figure out what background sounds work best for you.

15

Sensory Overload

The flip side of sensory deprivation is sensory overload. Too many things coming at you all at one time can overload your brain and shut it down.

Trying to watch television or a movie while writing doesn't net great results. Your brain can't concentrate on both simultaneously. That's why you'll hear "turn off the TV" repeated many times on writer's forums and videos. This is personally one of my biggest obstacles. I love movies so I try to write and watch at the same time. I find that I often sit back in my chair to watch the show, my writing forgotten.

And that is only two things conflicting at once for your time. When you add in chattering children, barking dogs, phone calls, work, home improvements, loud music, bills, research, advertisements, etc., it is easy to be overwhelmed and not able to focus on your writing. If you can't focus on your writing either your writing quality will suffer or it won't get done.

How do you beat becoming overloaded?

Well, the obvious answer is to **turn things off**. Turn off the television and turn off the radio.

Leave your phone in the other room. I have my phone with me almost all the time. I like to leave it on for emergencies but I find that if I have it with me I always feel it pulling at me. I want to look at it, especially with ringing, dinging and blinking notifications. The first few times I left it in another room I felt a bit naked. You get used to it and it is actually quite refreshing and empowering to not carry it all the time.

It will likely be difficult to leave your phone the first few times. Social media and smart phones are highly addictive, just like alcohol, cigarettes, gambling, and drugs, which all have age limits or are illegal (This is just one reason my daughters won't get their own phones until they are older!). The only difference is that smart phones are legal for anyone to use at any age. There is a wonderful video interview with Simon Sinek where he discusses *Millennials in the Workplace* that explains this amazingly well. He starts talking about cell phones around the three-minute mark but the whole interview is fascinating and worth watching. Link: https://tinyurl.com/yc7wr296.

Go someplace quiet to write like a library or perhaps a coffee shop or bookstore.

Get an ad-blocker app for your phone and computer. The less ads you see the less they can distract you. Remember, marketeers want you to notice their ads so they make it as difficult as they can for you to ignore them. Ads on the Internet are even targeted specifically to you based on your browsing and purchase history.

You can also get an app or program that will **lock-down your Internet** so that you can't use it for a specified period of time.

The main goal is to try to limit the never-ending barrage of things that are competing for your attention. You can't control everything but you can control your exposure to an extent.

16

No Support

Writing can be lonely, especially when you don't have people around you who support your choice or understand why you want to write or even what is involved. This can include friends, family, coworkers, acquaintances, or even social media friends. If no one is there to support you, to help you, everything seems harder and feels more like a chore than a fun activity. You may even feel like you "have to do this" in order to prove yourself to everyone else.

There are also varying levels of support. On a low support-level, take my wife, for example. She is wonderful and I am thankful every day for her but I don't believe that she really understands my author-life. She understands my driving reasons and my dreams but she isn't a writer and doesn't even read the type of stories that I write. Still, she is supportive in her own way, at a minimalist level.

On a high-support level, by contrast, my writers' group has members who totally get it, that are in the same place that I am, and that have their own dreams of being a published author. They offer valuable critiques and ideas and some socialization and community. Since writing is primarily a solitary activity, those last two are extremely important.

In-between those, I also started a small lunch-time writing group at work. We don't talk too much during our time. We mostly just write. This is another form of community and support and it gives us all dedicated time to write. A double win!

I've been fortunate that I have been involved in writing groups for many years, but where can you find support in your own area?

Libraries often have writers' events posted. If not, you should be able to set one up yourself fairly easily for free. It may take a while to get a consistent core group but it will take even longer if you don't start it at all. Don't count on someone else to start one. They are waiting for you to do it. **Don't put your future on hold waiting for someone else to give you an opportunity. Make the opportunity yourself.**

Meetup.com also has a lot of writers' groups. Each group has its own description. Do a general search and pick the ones you want to join. Some groups have a join/annual fee, others don't. If you want to start your own group at Meetup.com, it will cost you around $180 a year if you are in the U.S.

Another good place to get support is on-line list-serves. Yahoo Groups and Google+ both have a lot of groups you can join. You'll get periodic emails when messages are posted. Some of these groups hold contests or critique sessions and offer valuable information on publishing and many other writing-related topics which can help you.

You can also count on social media for support. Facebook not only has lots of writing groups but you can also talk to your extended friend-base about writing related issues. They will be happy to share their opinions.

You can ask around at work to see if anyone is interested in writing a book.

There are many places you can look for support. It's just a matter of knowing where to start. **Once you find one good source of support more opportunities will present themselves.**

17

Complacency

Perhaps you've already written and published a book. Congratulations if you have! Now is not the time to relax though. You need to follow that book with another one and then another one. Your audience needs to know that you are going to bring them consistent stories.

Even if you haven't published yet, you might still slip into a complacent state and stop trying harder. You may achieve your base goal and that is enough for you. Yay! You reached your goal. Now you can relax, right? Well, technically you can, but why should you?

Let's say that you have a goal of writing for an hour each day. You've reached that goal every day for a few weeks. You tell yourself that what you are doing is awesome, and it is, but what if you pushed your goal even higher? What if you tried to write for 90 minutes a day instead?

What if you didn't? What if you decided that you were happy with one hour every day? You have reached a comfortable goal and have become complacent. You feel good because you are reaching your short-term goal of writing for an hour each day. Why should you leave that comfort zone and attempt more, which is likely to be painful in the short-term?

The reason in this example is because you only have the short-term goals so that you can reach you long-term goal of writing a book. Will you book get written at an hour a day? Certainly, but it you pushed yourself a little harder, say thirty extra minutes a day, your book could be finished and making you money even faster. Thirty minutes is a TV sitcom.

Here are a few examples. We'll estimate that you can write 500 words in an hour which is well within your grasp. My maximum typing speed is around 45 words per minute and I can get about 500 "good" words in 30 minutes even with editing-as-I-go. I know people who can type upwards of 120 words per minute. We'll also estimate that your book will be 70,000 words long, which is standard for a lot of genres. In complacent mode: 1 hour a day = 500 words. 70,000/500 = 140 days or 4.66 months. Pushing your goal and yourself: 90 minutes a day = 750 words. 70,000/750 = 93.33 days or 3.1 months.

Wow! Just by pushing yourself an extra 30 minutes a day, or 250 more words, you can shave a month and a half off your time. That is a month and a half sooner that you can start selling your story.

And imagine if you only write one or two days a week right now. If you stepped up and started writing three or four days a week you could cut your time in half.

Focus on the big goal. See if there is someplace where you have become complacent, someplace where you can push yourself a little harder. Not only will you reach your long-term goal faster but you will feel better about yourself because you pushed yourself past where you thought your limits were.

18

Over Researching

There are times when every writer needs to research something. You might need to know what kind of tree should be in your story setting or how long a person can be choked before they pass out. Details can be part of what makes your story great so knowing the facts is paramount.

You get in trouble when you begin to over research. Maybe you find out that pine trees are predominant in the area of your setting. But then you decide that a little more detail couldn't hurt, so you delve deeper. You decide to learn about the properties of the bark, the effect of the seasons on the trees, what bugs live on the trees, and what the wood it provides is used for specifically. This is all great information, but most of it is unlikely to make it into your story. Naturally, if you are writing a non-fiction book, then more facts are necessary but you can still over research.

Now you have used more time for research than for writing. And a lot of what you've researched probably won't ever go into your story. That's not to say that information isn't valuable. It totally is. As a writer you probably know more back-story on your characters in order to understand them better than what actually gets into your books.

However, there is a fine line between knowing tidbits of information that will likely serve you better in Trivial Pursuit than in your story and knowing the general information that the readers need in order to be able to extrapolate into their own lives.

If over-researching is one of your obstacles, there are a few things you can do. One idea is to set up a specific "researching" time much like you might set up a specific "writing" time. In that way, you can do research separately from your actual writing so that your writing time is not compromised and will be more productive.

You could also set a timer on your research. If you need to stop writing to look something up, set a timer for 3-5 minutes and then go back to writing. That will help you focus on getting back to what is more important - the writing. You can't share your story with other people if it doesn't get written.

19

Fatigue

Are you tired? I'm often tired. I don't get enough sleep. I find it difficult to get to bed early despite having good intentions every day. There is always one more thing to do, one more "I'll go to bed after I do this" moment, one more thing to peak my interest. I read headlines all the time about how sleep deprivation is an epidemic so I know that I'm not alone.

Other than the obvious answer of going to bed earlier, what can you do about it?

This may seem counter-intuitive but **regular exercise can help**. Exercise will give you more energy and make you emotionally happier. Yes, after a workout you might be exhausted, but later in the day or the next day you will reap the benefits. The more energy you have the less tired you are - that's just common sense.

Another option would be to **take power naps**. A power nap is different from an ordinary nap. For an ordinary nap you lie down somewhere comfortable and sleep as long as you want or have time to spare. I take this kind of nap sometimes. It always helps but it isn't as effective as a power nap.

A power nap has a few key elements. First, you need to lie down somewhere that is not as comfortable as you would like. It should be borderline uncomfortable or fully uncomfortable. When I was in college I used to lie down on the floor when I took them. When I worked two full-time jobs I would nap sitting up in a chair or in my car. Second, set a timer for 20-25 minutes before starting. Do not nap longer than 25 minutes. Once you go longer than that, the nap resets your internal sleep-cycle clock and tricks your body into thinking that you need more sleep. A power nap can be a great tool to have more energy to get you through the day.

As a rule, getting more sleep is better. Less sleep affects your health, your short-term memory, your ability to cope emotionally to situations, and so many other aspects. I know it is difficult. Even though I know all the bad things associated with sleep deprivation I still succumb to fatigue a lot due to not enough sleep and my short-term memory is awful. I used to think it was all the marijuana I used to smoke but now I think it is related to years of not getting enough sleep.

Take care of yourself. Treat yourself to some good, solid sleep.

20

Time

"I don't have enough time."

"I'm too busy."

"I've got too much to do."

"My family takes up a lot of my time."

Sound familiar? No one ever seems to have enough time. We are busy. That's a fact of life. But consider... **you have exactly the same amount of time each day as all of the great people in history and today**.

Albert Einstein created the Theory of Relativity and was awarded the Nobel Prize for Physics.

Leonardo da Vinci was an artist, scientist, and inventor and gave us two of the most iconic paintings in modern history, the Mona Lisa and The Last Supper.

Joan of Arc led a French army against the English during the Hundred Years War. At age sixteen she campaigned to King Charles of France for her army, and she helped him regain his throne before the age of nineteen. She was proclaimed a Saint of the Catholic church nearly 500 years after her death.

Saint Mother Teresa devoted her entire life to helping the poor, the sick, the helpless, and the needy. She was awarded the Nobel Peace Prize and formed the Missions of Charity which now has over 4,000 nuns who continue her work.

Arnold Schwarzenegger won five Mr. Universe titles and six Mr. Olympia crowns as a professional bodybuilder. Then he went on to become a major motion picture star starring in many iconic films. He also went on to become the Governor of the state of California in the United States.

Piers Anthony is an English American science fiction and fantasy author. So far during his career, he has published 166 works encompassing non-fiction books, novels, novellas, short stories, collections, and book series (through December 2013).

Robert Heinlein was an American science fiction writer and was often called the "dean of science fiction writers". During his life, he published 32 novels, 59 short stories, and 16 collections. Created from his stories were television shows, movies, radio shows, and even a board game.

How did those people and many others accomplish so much? They didn't have any more time than you. **What they did have was a vision and a drive to achieve it. They chose to pursue their vision over other things.**

As a writer, you too have a vision. You have a story to tell. You just need to decide what is more important to you. Should you use your time watching a television show after dinner or should you write instead? **Look at your life for areas where you waste time, where you use your time in pursuit of something other than your goal.** Shave five minutes here and ten minutes there. I expect that you'll find that you suddenly do have enough time to write your book.

And, as something to look forward to, the more you write the easier it becomes. Issac Newton's First Law of Motion states that "an object at rest stays at rest and an object in motion stays in motion with the same speed and in the same direction unless acted upon by an unbalanced force."

In writer's terms, if you aren't writing you'll likely continue to not write, and a story being written will keep being written at the same pace unless you push a little harder to speed it up.

21
Writer's Block

We've all heard of writer's block - those times when you have no ideas and no inspiration. Most of us have probably claimed writer's block as a reason for not writing at one point or another. There has been a debate in recent years as to the validity of writer's block - is it real or imagined? Irregardless of the arguments, if it feels real to some people then it is real for them and we will still encounter it.

I do believe that we overuse the term though. If we are tired and can't get motivated to write we may incorrectly label it as writer's block. If we are overwhelmed or depressed we may not be in the mindset to write but instead of labeling the problem correctly we call it writer's block. Mislabeling the symptom into the generalized writer's block category doesn't solve the underlying problem. It just gives you an easy excuse not to write.

The first thing you should do is **try to find an underlying cause for your inability to write**. If you can't identify one, or if you can identify one but can't fix it right now for some reason, then there are some things you can do to try to jump-start your writing, much like jump-starting a car - one good jolt to the battery and it runs like new again. Once you get some inertia going, it will become easier.

What are some things that you can do to get yourself writing again?

Exercise is always good. It gets your blood flowing into your brain and shoots you full of adrenaline. Go for a hike in the woods, or canoe on a lake, or play volleyball (that's what I do the most!), or even just walk around the neighborhood or rake some leaves in your yard. And not only will it get you away from your computer for a while but it will make you feel better about yourself too. Nice bonuses.

Try writing something different. **Choose a different story line or a new topic.** It will lead your thoughts down new avenues and may help you start again.

Go to a bar or other public place and sit and **watch people**. Try to make up stories about their lives as you perceive them. Maybe that guy is an abusive father; maybe that girl is the high school prom queen; perhaps that couple are trying to have a baby. The idea is to help your mind start thinking creatively again.

Pick a topic that interests you. One that I might pick would be non-verbal communication. Now write down ten to fifteen questions related to that topic. Then answer them yourself. This could give you a whole new book idea as well as get you writing again.

Join a writers' group. You cannot underestimate the value of other writer's feedback, conversation, and similar goals. And you have to go to meetings and actually talk to people. In the writer's group that I run, we have over 1,600 members but only a small portion of those members are active at any one time. I'd estimate 100 or less. That means around 1,500 people have aspirations of being a writer but don't reap any benefits after joining. Don't be that person.

Enter a short story or poetry contest that has a defined topic. The defined topic is important because it limits you and your natural tendency is to fight against those limits. I once entered a contest where the topic was "dark glass" and it led me to create one of the most unique worlds that I have ever written.

Pick a random photo on-line and tell a story about it.

Ask your friends about their saddest time, funniest story, or craziest idea they've had. Listening to them might give you ideas or focus.

Unplug. Put your phone down, turn off your television and computer, mute your radios. Go to the quietest, most secluded, place you can find like a beach or park bench and sit alone with just you and your thoughts. Don't focus on your writer's block. Just be in the moment of technical freedom. Try it for longer than a few minutes, maybe a half hour or an hour. People need time to introspect, and we don't often get it when surrounded by technology and screens.

Those are just some ideas. Hopefully, if you can get your fingers writing or typing again, even if it isn't on your target piece, it will get you past the mental hump of "I can't" and start you back on the correct path of "I can".

22
Negativity

Emotions are infectious. They can be passed from person to person like a cold. While some emotions like joy and excitement are positive and good, negativity is not one of those beneficial ones. If you get enough exposure to negativity you can catch it too. It gradually creeps in and infects your life.

I find that even though I feel I am an optimistic person, I say many negative things that I don't remember saying afterwards. I must have gotten at least some of that from my time with my ex-wife who was a negative person when I was with her. My current wife is helpful in pointing out times that I am being negative. It helps me focus on it and try to pay attention to how I act and what I say. I certainly don't want my children to become negative because of me.

How can negativity affect you as a writer?

It wears you down little by little, sapping you of energy and creativity. It causes you to look for what is wrong instead of what is right. Instead of focusing on how your story does work, you focus on what is wrong with it. Is your story awful because there is so much wrong with it or is it amazing because there is so much good in it?

Sometimes even the words you choose in your stories reflect negativity. An example might be: "He could not fly. It was too hard." versus "He tried to fly but found it difficult to flap his arms fast enough." The first one has your character stopping because he had negative thinking as opposed to the second one that had your character trying first and then failing for another reason.

You may be negative when in a writers' group and they might start distancing themselves from you out of discomfort. They may end up valuing your input or critiques less or instead of giving you valuable feedback, they might catch the negativity too and only offer negative feedback on your stories.

One tool that I've found to help combat negativity is *The Five Minute Journal* created by Alex Ikonn and UJ Ramdas (see Appendix 2 for link). It is around US$20.00. Each page has an inspirational quote and five brief fill-in-the-blanks sections, three for in the morning and two for before bed. You just fill in the sections every day first thing in the morning and last thing at night. It doesn't even take five minutes most days.

The morning sections are:

- "I am grateful for..."
- "What would make today great?"
- "Daily affirmations. I am..."

The evening sections are:

- "3 Amazing things that happened today."
- "How could I have made today better."

I was a skeptical when I started, but I have noticed a definite increase in optimism and decline in pessimism after doing it daily for a while. I've been doing it for around five months now. It has surprised me how many things I am grateful for, and, while there are a few repeats, most days I can find three new things.

And I can feel my **daily affirmation** as part of me now rather than just words or an idea. "I am a writer. I am confident and strong. I will publish." Writing it every day has etched it into my brain.

To be honest, you could make the *Five Minute Journal* yourself in MS Word, however, I find it convenient and easier just to purchase one that is already put together, rather than wasting time making my own. In that way, I don't need to worry about setup, printing, or wanting to fill it out it on the computer. Part of the reason it works is because you hand write it which helps it sink into your subconscious more than typing it. Plus, it is a quality book, not a mass market paperback.

Exercise is also a great way to combat negativity. When you exercise, chemicals are released into your brain that actually improve your mood. Exercise boosts your confidence and raises your self esteem. That's probably why I enjoy volleyball so much. It makes me feel good and gives me more energy.

Set some small, easy goals and then complete them. When you accomplish something you feel better about yourself. Don't make them fluff goals either. They need to have real merit. Setting a goal of making a cup of tea by 6 o'clock is empty. Your subconscious will know and you won't feel any real accomplishment. Pick something like turning off the television and writing for twenty minutes. When you complete small, attainable goals like that, you'll feel better and more positive.

23

Endless Ideas

Having creative ideas is great. Having a lot of them is also great. They are the starting point for all your stories. So, why is there a chapter on having too many ideas then?

One downside that I've noticed about having too many ideas is that I have a desire to write about all of them at once. I put one story down, pick up another, and then switch to a third. My excitement and energy carry along with each switch, which takes them away from the first or second story.

In other words, I lose focus and pleasure on the first story because I am now writing something newer and more exciting to me. I often do not go back to the first story to finish writing it either because I've lost the story-line or "feel" of the story or because it doesn't excite me anymore.

For example, right now I am working on four separate projects: this book, a children's picture book series, a sci-fi short story, and an adult coloring book, and there are still more ideas brewing. Each one of these is in a different stage and needs just a little more to be completed. It has been difficult for me to finish this book. I keep wanting to move on to something else. I want to write, not create audio books or draw illustrations or book covers. Yes, those can be outsourced for a fee but I am trying to save a little money too (aren't we all!).

Maybe the best way to beat having too many ideas competing for your time is to **finish what you are working on first**. Write your ideas down in one central location rather than trying to flesh them out too much.

Don't outline the entire story when you first have the idea. Write down just enough key points to remind you of the thrust of your idea later.

Nearly everyone has heard this saying before: "Jack of all trades, master of none." If you are writing ten different stories at once, you mind and effort are divided in ten different directions at once. You need to commit to one, or only a few, stories at a time. **The most important thing if you want to publish is to finish your story**.

24

Burnout

I added this chapter a year after the rest of this book had been written. I finished the book thirteen months ago and had the edits completed a month after that.

I was working on several other projects at the same time. I was working long days and sleeping short nights for about six months straight. My job turned into ten months of non-stop, high-intensity hell and I wanted to quit it many times. My time at home also became busier as my daughters kept right on growing. I started to lose focus, and then energy, and then desire to write and publish my books.

I burned out. I crashed hard and didn't accomplish much for almost a year.

I still wrote every day because of my Don't Break the Chain calendar but I mostly wrote small amounts, less than a paragraph, and they were on projects that I wasn't fully invested in. I needed something easy to write, something that didn't take brain power, just to make my daily writing goal. But, outside of my daily writing, I didn't accomplish much towards publishing my book. It is only now that I am starting to find focus again and am able to move forward.

Burnout doesn't just happen overnight. Stress, overwork, and sleep deprivation slowly wear on you until your mind shuts down. You can't function effectively and your personal or professional life may suffer. You are emotionally and physically exhausted. You become negative and detached. You feel ineffective and have no sense of accomplishment. You become forgetful or lack concentration. Maybe your appetite suffers or you become more anxious or depressed. There are many symptoms and signs of burnout.

But how can you beat burnout?

Disconnect. Make time to get away from your projects. Leave your work at the office if possible. Take time off to refocus and recharge.

I haven't read the entire Stephen Covey book *The Seven Habits of Highly Effective People*. The biggest take away I got from that book was "sharpen the saw." Imagine that you are sawing a big log into pieces with a new wood saw. The first cut goes quickly. The second cut is a little slower because the saw has been dulled by the first cut. The third cut takes even longer and now you have to work the saw harder because it has been dulled even more. By the time you get several more slices into the log your saw has become completely dull and you need to exert even more pressure and strength to make the cut and it takes a lot more time to saw completely through the log than the first cut. However, if you take a break from sawing the logs and take a few minutes to sharpen the saw then it will cut better again, faster and with less effort. **Take some time away from your stress and projects to sharpen your own saw**. You'll be more productive and effective.

Another important way to combat burnout is to get sleep. **Go to bed** at night. Don't force yourself to stay awake to do "just one more" thing. I'm guilty of doing that. Give your brain time to process things and rest. Also, try not to take sleeping pills or medicine like Nyquil or Valium to help you sleep, and steer clear of alcohol and recreational drugs too. Any of these will disrupt your body's natural sleep cycle.

Take regular breaks at work or during the day. **Schedule breaks** or time to relax if you can't seem to find extra time. That's a similar principle as paying yourself first. I read once that you should always set aside money for yourself by treating yourself as a bill that needs to be paid first. So I would pay the "Ed Gold" bill of $25-50 every paycheck and then pay the rest of my bills. That way I keep something for myself rather than putting all my hard-earned money into someone else's pocket. Scheduling official time for breaks works the same way. It sets time aside so you can take care of yourself before taking care of work that will still be there 15 or 20 minutes later. Work will always be there. Your health may not.

Get organized. Clean your workspace. Tidy your house. Clutter puts extra stress on your mind and eyes just to sort through the mess. Plus, it also makes it more difficult to find things when you need them which also adds to stress. Any stress you can remove will help battle burnout.

Pay attention to what your body is telling you. If you are falling asleep in inappropriate situations, like driving, lunchtime at work, or sitting and doing something calm, you may not be getting enough sleep. If you can't concentrate or get impatient or grumpy easily you may be overstressed. Your body knows what it needs most of the time. You just need to listen to it.

Also, **spend time with your friends and family**. Lean on people who care about you for support. This will help you not only have some fun but will also remove you from your stressors and can help prevent burnout.

Regarding Obstacles to Publishing

An early reader pointed out that they would have liked a chapter on publishing.

When I started writing this book it's main focus was on self-publishing and the obstacles portion was just going to be a brief section. However, as I started writing, I realized that the obstacles deserved their own book. I set aside the publishing portion to focus on providing ideas for overcoming obstacles that we all face.

The obstacles in this book are more abstract and require self-evaluation, perseverance, and often long-term changes. Obstacles to publishing are more concrete, like where to publish, how to publish, what format(s) to use, finding buyers, and designing covers and illustrations, to name a few.

So, while publishing is certainly important and another huge part of being an author, I opted to exclude it from this book since it is a topic unto itself and doesn't fit with this book's theme.

Conclusion

I laid myself bare on these pages. Some of the chapters were hard to share because they were personal and involved shooting myself with an x-ray gun. I learned a lot about myself though and the general writing process as well. I also encountered every single one of these obstacles while writing this book.

There are many obstacles that you will face but there are also many solutions you can implement to overcome them. Sometimes the obstacle will win, sometimes you'll win. All you need to do is continue trying and not give up. Wars are never won in just one battle, or without casualties.

I hope that this book has given you some ideas on how to overcome common obstacles that you will face as a writer and that my personal experiences help you realize that you are not alone. Every one of us has similar situations in our lives.

Good luck and I'd be interested in hearing any comments, stories, or solutions that you have.

> Alice came to a fork in the road. "Which road do I take?" she asked.
>
> "Where do you want to go?" responded the Cheshire cat.
>
> "I don't know," Alice answered.
>
> "Then," said the cat, "it doesn't matter."
>
> — **Lewis Carroll,** *Alice in Wonderland*

Appendix 1
People Mentioned

This is a list of some of the people I referenced in this book, along with their information, to make it easier for you to follow or contact them.

Jeff Goins *(Motivation)*
   Website: *goinswriter.com*
   "I write books and help writers get their work out into the world. I am the best-selling author of five books, including *The Art of Work*. Each week, I send out a newsletter with free tips on writing and creativity." (from Jeff's website)

Joanna Penn *(Motivation)*
   Website: *http://www.JFPenn.com*
   Podcast: *www.TheCreativePenn.com/podcast*
      FREE Author 2.0 Blueprint: *www.TheCreativePenn.com/blueprint*
   New York Times and *USA Today* bestselling thriller author. Speaker. Entrepreneur.

Tara Lynn Groth, Freelance Writer *(Motivation)*
   Website: *www.taralynnegroth.com*
   Website: *www.writenaked.net*
   Tara Lynne Groth's articles have appeared in magazines and newspapers for more than a decade. She has written for trade and consumer publications including *GRIT*, *Produce Business*, *Blue Ridge Country*, *Durham News*, and more.

James Clear *(Motivation)*
Website*: JamesClear.com*
James Clear writes at JamesClear.com, where he shares self-improvement tips based on proven scientific research. You can read his best articles or join his free newsletter to learn how to build habits that stick.

Bryan Harris *(Motivation)*
Website*: http://videofruit.com*
"I've made 100's of videos for myself and other people. I love teaching other people how to make killer videos for their business. [My] blog is a place you can learn about how to USE and to MAKE video in your business." (from website)

Jon Bard *(Motivation)*
Website*: http://writeforkids.org*
"The core of our business is the same as it always has been*: Children's Book Insider, the Newsletter for Children's Writers. Every month, for more than two decades, we've shared instruction, advice, market tips and inspiration through the pages of the CBI.* We're proud to be known as the source for all aspiring and working children's writers." (from website)

Anthony Robbins *(Self Esteem, Over Preparation, Procrastination)*
Website*: https://www.tonyrobbins.com*
Tony Robbins is an entrepreneur, best-selling author, philanthropist and the nation's #1 Life and Business Strategist. A recognized authority on the psychology of leadership, negotiations and organizational turnaround, he has served as an advisor to leaders around the world for more than 38 years. (from website)

Appendix 2
Products Mentioned

This is a list of some of the products I referenced in this book, along with their information, to make it easier for you to locate them.

Disclaimer: I am an affiliate for Learn Scrivener Fast and Self Publishing School. However, that in no way affects what you would pay to buy those services nor does it mean that I am praising them for monetary gain. I believe they are both high-quality products and worth investigating. It does, however, mean that if you buy through my link, I'll earn a commission on your purchase. So, if you decide you like either of those enough to purchase them, I'd be grateful if you could use my links. Thank you so much!

FREE Writer's Don't Break the Chain Calendar (*Procrastination*)
Edward Gold
Website: *http://www.edwardgold.com/free-writers-chain-calendar/*
To receive your free printable copy of this calendar by email,
please visit: *http://www.edwardgold.com/Obstacles-FG-calendar*
Use this one-page calendar to track your daily "chain" of accomplished goals, along with your word count.

Scrivener (by Literature and Latte) (*Boredom*)
Website: *http://www.literatureandlatte.com/scrivener.php*
Scrivener is a software program developed specifically for writers and makes non-linear writing a breeze. You can download and use the full, unlimited software free for 30 days, and the 30 days is not linear/consecutive. It is 30 actual/non-consecutive days. For Windows or Mac.

Learn Scrivener Fast (*Boredom*)
  Joseph Michael
  Website*: http://learnscrivenerfast.com*
  Affiliate Link*: https://kb226.isrefer.com/go/lsfsp/EdwardGold*
    "Joseph Michael is a top-notch Scrivener coach who helps people become world-class writers by mastering Scrivener. His online course, Learn Scrivener Fast, has helped even best-selling authors and full-time writers create their best work." (from website)

Self-Publishing School (*Perfectionism*)
  Chandler Bolt
  Website*: https://self-publishingschool.com*
  Affiliate Link*: https://xe172.isrefer.com/go/sps4fta-vts/EdwardGold*
    "There's a book inside you. And my goal is to help you find it and go from blank page to bestseller – even if you're busy, idea-less, or bad at writing like me... You just need a proven system and strategies to beat overwhelm and guide you from blank page to bestseller." (from website)

The Five Minute Journal (*Negativity*)
  On website*: http://www.fiveminutejournal.com*
  On Amazon*: http://amzn.to/2uHWway*
    "Using the science of positive psychology to improve happiness, The Five Minute Journal focuses your attention on the good in your life. Improve your mental well-being and feel better every day." (from Amazon)

Sunrise Earth (*Sensory Deprivation*)
  On YouTube: *Search for "Sunrise Earth", full episodes are about 52 minutes.*
  On Amazon: *http://amzn.to/2uHNytC (Seaside Collection, or search for "Sunrise Earth" for more choices)*
    "Sunrise Earth focused on presenting the viewer with sunrises in various geographical locations throughout the world. It is also notable for its complete lack of human narration, concentrating instead on the natural sounds of each episodes' specific location. High-definition video and Dolby 5.1 stereo surround sound are used to present each natural environment in a clear and detailed manner." (from Wikipedia) There are 64 episodes total.

Millennials in the Workplace YouTube Video (*Sensory Overload*)
YouTube: *https://tinyurl.com/yc7wr296*
Simon Sinek discusses the Millennial generation and how cell phones affect us.

About the Author

Edward Gold is a science fiction and fantasy author and he also writes children's books. He has won contests for his short stories and has published several poems. He is the organizer of a local writers' group with over 1,500 members. He has also produced, designed, and edited newsletters for several agencies and literary magazines.

He likes hiking and playing volleyball. He has organized and captained many volleyball teams in the past, and he still plays sand-doubles almost every week. In addition, he enjoys photography, movies, books, walleyball, games, karaoke, and spending time with his family.

He likes to travel and experience new things and has been to many domestic and international destinations, including Africa, Canada, London and the Caribbean. So far, he has lived in or visited 24 of the 50 states in the U.S.

He currently lives in Durham, North Carolina, with his wife, his two daughters, and their boxer-bulldog.

You may reach Edward Gold in the following ways:

Main website: *www.EdwardGold.com*
Facebook: *https://www.facebook.com/Edward-Gold-1104765112885690/*
Twitter: *https://twitter.com/EdwardGoldSFF*
Goodreads: *https://www.goodreads.com/user/show/1090482-edward-gold*